# Redesigning
# Learning Spaces

CORWIN
CONNECTED
EDUCATORS
SERIES

# Redesigning Learning Spaces

**Robert Dillon**

**Ben Gilpin**

**A.J. Juliani**

**Erin Klein**

CORWIN
A SAGE Publishing Company

FOR INFORMATION:

Corwin

A SAGE Company

2455 Teller Road

Thousand Oaks, California 91320

(800) 233–9936

www.corwin.com

SAGE Publications Ltd.

1 Oliver's Yard

55 City Road

London EC1Y 1SP

United Kingdom

SAGE Publications India Pvt. Ltd.

B 1/I 1 Mohan Cooperative Industrial Area

Mathura Road, New Delhi 110 044

India

SAGE Publications Asia-Pacific Pte. Ltd.

3 Church Street

#10–04 Samsung Hub

Singapore 049483

Printed in the United States of America

ISBN 978-1-5063-1831-8

This book is printed on acid-free paper.

Acquisitions Editor:   Ariel Bartlett

Editorial Assistant:   Andrew Olson

Production Editor:   Amy Schroller

Copy Editor:   Michelle Ponce

Typesetter:   C&M Digitals (P) Ltd.

Proofreader:   Bonnie Moore

Cover and Interior Designer:   Janet Kiesel

Marketing Manager:   Anna Mesick

Certified Chain of Custody
SUSTAINABLE   Promoting Sustainable Forestry
FORESTRY   www.sfiprogram.org
INITIATIVE   SFI-01268
SFI label applies to text stock

16 17 18 19 20 10 9 8 7 6 5 4 3 2 1

# Contents

# Preface

M y best friend is a high school math teacher. When I started working with Peter on the Corwin Connected Educators series, I excitedly told her about the power of using social media to connect with other educators. I passed on what I learned from the authors in this series: that the greatest resource educators have is each other. At a conference, she heard Jennie Magiera speak and finally made the leap to getting on Twitter. Although I wasn't sure she would continue tweeting, she did, and even joined Twitter chats like #connectedtl and #slowmathchat. A few days later, she texted me saying, "I seriously cannot thank you enough. You have changed my life."

Being "connected" seems deceptively simple: Just get on Twitter, right? But that's really not enough. For those who truly embrace connectedness, it's a lifestyle change, an openness to sharing and learning in an entirely new environment. We're seeing the impact of this shift in mindset worldwide. Policies are changing, new jobs in education are being created, hitherto impossible collaborations are happening, pedagogy is evolving, and there's a heightened awareness of each person's individual impact. All of these changes are explored in the Connected Educators series.

While you can see the full list of books on the series page, we've introduced several new books to the series; they published in the fall of 2015 and spring of 2016. These books each contribute something unique and necessary not only for educators who are new to the world of connected education but also for those who have been immersed in it for some time.

Tom Whitby, coauthor of *The Relevant Educator,* has brought together a group of experienced connected educators in his new book, *The Educator's Guide to Creating Connections.* Contributors Pam Moran, George Couros, Kyle Pace, Adam Bellow, Lisa Nielsen, Kristen Swanson, Steven Anderson, and Shannon McClintock Miller discuss the ways that connectedness has impacted them and the benefits it can have for all educators—policy makers, school and district leaders, and teachers.

While all connected educators are evangelists for being connected, connectedness does not necessarily prevent common problems, such as isolation in leadership. In *Breaking Out of Isolation,* Spike Cook, Jessica Johnson, and Theresa Stager explain how connectedness can alleviate the loneliness leaders can feel in their position and also, when used effectively, help leaders maintain balance in their lives and stay motivated.

For districts and schools embracing the connected mindset and empowering all of their learners to use technology, a solid plan for digital citizenship is a must. In *Digital Citizenship,* Susan M. Bearden provides a look at how leaders can prepare teachers and students for the new responsibilities of using technology and interacting with others on a truly global platform.

Connected education provides unique opportunities for teachers in their classrooms as well. In *Standing in the Gap,* Lisa Dabbs and Nicol R. Howard explore the ways that social media can specifically help new teachers find resources, connect to mentors, and encourage each other in their careers. Robert Dillon, Ben Gilpin, A.J. Juliani, and Erin Klein show how teachers can purposefully integrate technology and empower their students in both physical and digital classrooms in *Redesigning Learning Spaces.*

One of the most powerful impacts connected education can have is in reaching marginalized populations. In *Confident Voices,* John Spencer shows how social media and other technology tools can empower English language learners. Billy Krakower and Sharon LePage Plante have also discovered that technology can reach special and gifted learners as well.

The books in the Corwin Connected Educators series are supported by a companion website featuring videos, articles, downloadable forms, and other resources to help you as you start and continue your journey. Best of all, the authors in the series want to connect with *you!* We've provided their Twitter handles and other contact information on the companion website.

Once you've taken the step to joining a network, don't stop there. Share what you're doing; you never know when it will help someone else!

*—Peter M. DeWitt, Series Editor*
@PeterMDeWitt

*—Ariel Bartlett, Acquisitions Editor*
@arielkbartlett

# About the Authors

**Robert Dillon** serves the students and community of the Affton School District as director of technology and innovation. Prior to this position, he served as a teacher and administrator in public schools throughout the St. Louis area. Dr. Dillon has a passion to change the educational landscape by building excellent engaging schools for all students. He looks for ways to ignite positive risk taking in teachers and students and release trapped wisdom into the system by growing networks of inspired educators. Dr. Dillon has had the opportunity to speak throughout the country at local, state, and national conferences as well as share his thoughts and ideas in a variety of publications. He is supported by his wife, Sandra and two daughters, Emily and Ellie. Dr. Dillon is also an avid runner, reader, and cyclist.

**Ben Gilpin** is the principal at Warner Elementary in the Western School District. Warner Elementary is located in Spring Arbor, Michigan. He is a student-centered educator who is focused on collaboration, teamwork, student engagement, and leadership.

Gilpin is all about the whole child; he cares deeply about all of his students, and he always tries to foster caring and impactful relationships. Ben began his career teaching fifth grade. After nine years in the classroom, he accepted a position as principal in the Western School District.

He has taken an active role in sharing his school's story. He understands the importance of spreading a positive message to the entire community.

Gilpin is viewed as an innovative leader throughout Jackson County and the State of Michigan. Ben was recently named one of the Top 100 Influential Voices of 2014 by Bam Radio. He has also presented and consulted on numerous educational topics. Most recently, Ben led sessions on Twitter, Professional Blogging, Personalized Learning, and Redesigning Learning Spaces.

Gilpin earned his elementary education degree from Tri-State University, his master's in education from Spring Arbor University and his Educational Leadership Certificate from Eastern Michigan University. To learn more about Ben's work, visit: http://colorful principal.blogspot.com or www.BenGilpin.com, or connect with Ben on Twitter at @benjamingilpin.

**A.J. Juliani** is the education and technology innovation specialist for Upper Perkiomen School District and co-founder of the ClassroomCribs.com site. Juliani is the author of *Learning by Choice* and *Inquiry and Innovation in the Classroom*. Learn more about A.J. on his blog at ajjuliani.com.

**Erin Klein** is an award-winning educator, national keynote speaker, author, and mother who has been twice selected to serve on the Scholastic, Inc. Top Teaching Team based in New York. Her recent publication, *Amazing Grades,* was a collaboration with experts from thirteen countries around the world. She travels the country speaking about the power of student voice, how meaningful technology integration can enhance learning experiences, and the impact classroom design has on today's learner.

She is certified in Brain Gym, Educational Kinesiology, and has studied under consultants from The Center for Effective Learning to understand how design affects cognition and learning. Klein serves as a classroom design consultant and creative partner for the publishing company, Carson-Dellosa. Some of her articles and interviews on design for education and technology tools for the classroom can be found on Smartblogs for Education, MindShift, Scholastic, Edudemic, Edutopia, EdSurge, and EdReach.

Klein served for the past three years as the state's technology chairperson for the Michigan Reading Association and is the 2014 recipient of the MACUL PreK–12 Teacher of the Year for Michigan. In 2013, Klein was also awarded her district's Teacher of the Year award. She currently serves on the advisory board for Remind101 in San Francisco and is an organizer for the EdCamp Detroit Annual Educational unConference. Among Klein's accomplishments, she was also recognized as a SMART Technologies Exemplary Educator, International Society for Technology in Education (ISTE) 2012 Social Media Influencer, a National Association of Independent Schools Teacher of the Future, ASCD Emerging Leader, and a member of The National Writing Project. This past summer, Klein was accepted into The Teacher's College at Columbia University to advance her studies in reading and writing workshop.

Klein has also hosted webinars for The United States Department of Education to share her perspective on Future Ready Schools. Most recently she was one of nine professionals selected to be a featured speaker on Future Ready Schools at the national Digital Learning Day in Washington DC.

For the past two years, Klein has been invited to Washington DC to represent the BAM 100 Influential Voice in Education. In 2014, Klein was selected to serve on the state of Michigan's Voice Fellowship, through America Achieves. Through this initiative, she was invited to be a part of the national Teach to Lead summits through The National Board for Professional Teaching Standards and the United States Department of Education where she continues to work on shaping teacher leadership across the country.

She has her master's of Education in Curriculum and Instruction, currently teaches at the elementary level, and lives in Michigan with her family. Her work can be found on her award-winning educational blog, Kleinspiration.com, and you can follow her on Twitter @KleinErin.

# Introduction

Teachers everywhere are working harder, being pressed from all sides for results, and reacting to the initiative overload that has flooded the education horizon. This often has even the best teachers feeling like an oarless boat on a rocky ocean just surviving and reacting. What if this didn't have to be the case? What if there were a way not just to catch up, but also to leap ahead? What if there were a way to create the success that you entered the profession to carry out?

We believe that the profession that we love is inching closer to this being a reality. A combination of factors seems to be crashing together, bringing hope, joy, and positive energy back to the daily work in the classroom. These factors are shared resources and ideas, a deep desire for caring communities that tend to the whole child, and the incredible shifts that can happen in classroom design quickly and on a sustainable budget.

This book looks to focus on all three of these concepts, with its core being an exploration of how learning-space design can positively impact classroom learning, the culture of a school, healthy communities that wrap around kids, and the systems and structures that make education what it is.

Making this powerful change possible will depend on teachers envisioning their role in a multi-faceted way. We hope that teachers reading this book will see themselves as facilitators of deeper, quality learning, as learners and positive risk-takers for kids, and most important as empowered change agents who recognize the power and possibility of growing our system of learning, especially in the area of learning-space design, to new heights.

The chapters that follow ask more questions than provide answers, but the hope is to spark a conversation about how now is the time to turn one of the final bastions of traditional school—the learning space—on its head. We hope that this book provides you with valuable ideas and resources to persuade you to take up this charge and encourage others to follow.

It is time for the desks to lose and the children to win. Join us in exploring how learning-space design and transforming learning spaces can truly reorient schools and bring a greater sense of control, peace, and joy to the teachers who make our schools incredible places for kids.

CHAPTER

1

# Leading Change Through Classroom Learning-Space Design

## WHY CHANGE CLASSROOM SPACE NOW?

Designing learning spaces is foundational. As a teacher, you can have the best curriculum and you can be the best facilitator of knowledge, but if you don't have an environment that's conducive for learning, then nothing else truly matters. Imagine trying to learn something that is unfamiliar to you or trying something new for the first time. If these things are occurring in an environment that is overstimulating, noisy, or uncomfortable, it's like being at the bottom of Maslow's hierarchy because you don't feel comfortable or safe. The result will be that you are never able to reach any deep level of learning.

One of the first design principles that teachers should recognize as they design an optimal learning space is to start by talking to the students. They are the ones who will really define comfort and speak to its essential nature. They will talk about how certain seating arrangements in the room make them feel more comfortable. These listening sessions help teachers to see and hear the links between comfort and learning. This is true for adults as well. Comfort also creates more stamina for the current task at hand.

> **Start a classroom redesign by talking to the students.**

Great community examples showcase what is possible for the classroom. Places that are learner-centered, engaging, and dynamic all provide clues to the optimal classroom experience. One example of this is a hands-on museum. These museums engage kids almost immediately. Just watch as kids hop inside of the bubble contraption; put their hands in the sand; or build, construct, and manipulate objects. In these environments, kids have tangible objects that allow them to become makers and creators. The environment builds a learning energy. It is essential to look for ways to make this a reality in the classroom as well. This means not confined or restricted in terms of bulky furniture that gets in the way. It means having enough space to collaborate and work with one another to solve problems.

*Children's museum*

Another space that can serve as an example for teachers looking to rethink their classrooms is a bookstore. Observe how comfortable kids are in the bookstore. They want to sit and linger and read books. Really take notice of the entire children's book section. Notice all of the children who are not with parents. There are no grownups. No one is teaching them. No one is telling them what to do, but they are actively engaged in self-selected books. In these spaces, you see children who have piles of books beside them and are just sitting and reading. Some are laying on floors. Some are on little beanbag chairs. Some are sitting across from one another in tables and chairs, and some are walking around shopping for books.

*Bookstore*

After seeing this, a teacher has to think that it is the most perfect example of a classroom and begin to ask questions like, "What elements that I observed are absent in my own classroom, and how can I integrate them into my classroom?" Classroom teachers seeing this scene would clearly want to infuse all of the dynamic learning that is happening, so that students could benefit from it every day.

## WHAT ARE OTHER EXPERTS SAYING ABOUT THE ELEMENTS OF LEARNING-SPACE DESIGN?

*research*

Interesting research on learning spaces was done by Carnegie Mellon University in regard to attention to allocation. They conducted two different studies on the amount of environmental print and the external stimulus that was in the classroom. Two different groups of learners were put in two different environments. One that was minimalistic in nature, and one that was very heavy on environmental print and external stimuli. When the children were given the same lesson and the same content delivered in the same methodology, the children in the minimalistic environment outperformed the children who were in the environment that was heavy on environmental print and stimuli. The conclusion to be drawn is that less in the classroom is truly more for learning (Carnegie Mellon University, 2014).

*clutter*

*\* key point*

Teachers who have started to take things down quickly realize how much it benefits kids. It allows the students to truly focus on the content that is being delivered rather than all of the busyness going on around the room. Susan Kovalik (n.d.) has also done research on colors and design, how to place objects in the room, how to arrange them, and how that affects cognition and learning for students. In regard to color, her research shows how more monotone, monochromatic colors from the same hue or palate, are better than the bright colors of red, yellow, and blue. Kovalik encourages teachers to use grays, tans, and browns and even maybe soft greens or soft blues.

*color*

_Technology Access_

When it comes to technology in the classroom, the optimal amount of technology in a space often depends on the classroom itself. Rarely does the device matter. It's all about how technology is being integrated by the teacher in the classroom. What is most important though is making sure that all students have access. This means that every classroom needs strong wireless access so that students can access resources and collaborate with one another and those beyond the walls of the classroom. There are a number of other smaller but essential components that go into setting up a successful learning space with technology, including having charging stations for devices and having enough power outlets to maintain classroom flexibility.

_Places of beauty_

It is also necessary for teachers to consider the importance of children learning in places of beauty. The importance of beauty in learning-space design can't be understated. Though beauty can be viewed as a subjective idea that varies for everyone, there are moments of universal beauty that stir all souls. Denis Dutton's (2010) TED talk, "A Darwinian theory of beauty," outlines this theory in more detail. He concludes that art, music, and other beautiful things, far from being simply "in the eye of the beholder," are a core part of human nature with deep evolutionary origins.

> Beauty is a core part of human nature.

Though it is great to "hack" learning spaces and add essential elements, it is important that students are exploring ideas, discovering connections, and debating issues in truly beautiful places to learn. Teachers who have already made these changes see how beauty contributes to learning in a deep and meaningful way. Beauty, for many children, is limited by their surroundings at home and in the community, so for these students, it is especially important that classrooms are also a place of beauty. (Beauty can push back against the effects of poverty) Beauty can stimulate new dreams. Beauty can facilitate connections to people, place, and planet. Teachers can be champions for learning spaces for a number of reasons, but one of the motives should be that beauty is good for learning, and all students need to experience beauty to grow to their potential.

# HOW DOES INTENTIONAL SPACE DESIGN IMPACT STUDENT MINDSET AND ATTITUDE?

*impact of learning spaces on learning*

As a way to help teachers see and feel the impact of learning spaces on learning, Erin shares some stories about how her classroom has come to life by using best practices around learning-space design.

It is interesting when students first see my learning space. They are not sure if it even is a classroom because it looks so far from the traditional space that they're used to. A corner breakfast nook is the first thing that they see, and beside it is a tall green plant. On the other side of the plant is a rocking chair. There is also a lot of natural light that minimizes the overhead fluorescent lighting. This helps to make the room feel calm. Seeing all of this, the students kind of peek in. Then when they actually come in, it is always interesting to hear those first sounds that they make. There are the sounds of wonder, excitement, and curiosity. Parents are also very curious. They say things like "Is this a classroom? What grade is this for?" Former students, who experienced the space before the redesign, make comments like, "Wow. Your room is so big," which is funny because my room is still quite small, very long and narrow, but after the redesign it appears so much larger.

One of my favorite comments that a student has ever made came when we were discussing what it means to have integrity and how proud I was of the class's behavior. One of the students just couldn't contain himself and said, "It's really easy. It's like whenever you walk into a McDonald's. You know it's just a place where you can have fun and run around and be crazy, but then when you go to a nice restaurant, you know to be on your best behavior. It's like that when we walk in our classroom, we know it's a space where we have to be respectful."

When teachers set the stage for success, students, just by peeking in, know that the learning space is an environment built and made for them. They know it is a serious place for learning. It is as though the teacher is saying, "I respect you as learners."(Classrooms designed with intention are very, very student centered, and created tastefully for kids. They are not spaces that you come into and see a bunch of teacher clutter that has been in binders for the past ten years.)

In excellently designed classrooms, students are not going to see a bunch of filing cabinets or items like laminated anchor charts plastered on the wall. Well-designed classrooms are filled with student-created materials. They have items that are brought down to the children's eye level. In the end, teachers should strive to build a classroom that has a family environment that is first and foremost comfortable for students.

Adjusting classroom libraries is another entry point for teachers who are looking to begin their journey around remaking their learning space. In places where kids are engaged with books in a deep way, the books are displayed so you can see all the spines without having to take some cumbersome bucket off of the shelf and dig through it. Ask kids if they want to redesign the classroom library, and they will most likely be ecstatic. Erin provides a great example of this from her classroom.

We took an entire day and took every book out of a bucket. I asked them how they wanted the books arranged and how they wanted to organize them. The students said that we should put them into categories. It was so nice to hear the kids have such a rich dialogue about, "Oh, I think that this is a mystery because . . . " The next thing that happened was that they began pulling more people into their conversation, and then there was this huge class debate about where particular books went.

It was such a meaningful conversation. It wasn't just, "Here's a worksheet, will you please match the title of this book to a genre you think it is?" They were actually doing something that was purposeful with meaning. They were doing something for themselves and for their classmates. It just had such purpose and a level of authenticity.

As seen from this example, central to the successful transformation of a classroom is a student-centered design process. Unfortunately, this is not the way that most decisions in classrooms are made. The voice of the student is often left behind. When there are only adults making decisions, issues surface that are seen as nonissues to the learners in the classroom. This can create a focus on the wrong issues resulting in money being spent on areas that fail to meet student needs. To avoid this, the design process needs to be bathed in empathy. In the case of classroom design, this empathy must include student voice on the essential elements of a modern learning experience. Teachers need to be asking questions like the following: When will students use these elements for learning? Will this engage students at a transformative level? Where can we take kids to experience a similar space for authentic feedback and observation?

Once the initial decisions have been made and the new space is taking shape, it remains essential for teachers and others in the school to stay dedicated to student voice. The daily experience of so many students is to show up, shut up, and shut down their devices. However, the best teachers are finding sustainable ways to promote student voice. One of the easiest symbols of supporting this mission is to enhance the writable space throughout the building by placing idea walls in classrooms, cafeterias, and hallways. Make desks, tables, and windows places where ideas and voice are seen and heard. It is amazing how seeing voice leads to hearing voice, so then voice can become part of the natural flow of a classroom and through a school.

## HOW SHOULD TEACHERS BEGIN THIS PROCESS?

Classroom redesign can often take place with little to no budget. Sure it may require bringing some new things to the classroom. This can be items from home, but even if you don't have access to extra items at home, there are items that can be acquired at garage sales or from Craigslist. There are also grant opportunities from parent organizations and a plethora of resources like Digital Wish

1st Step in learning space redesign

where you can apply for items for your classroom as well as DonorsChoose grants.

Beyond adding new things, it also doesn't cost a single penny to start minimizing the clutter in your room, taking items off of the wall, turning off the overhead, or pulling open the drapes. Just small changes, even bringing in a couple of plants from outside, can make a huge difference in making the classroom feel like a more comfortable learning space for kids.

Another way for teachers to showcase their commitment to change is to stop laminating items. It won't cost but rather actually save money. There are many other things that you can do as well. Be more intentional about how you post in the room, what you bring in, and how you arrange, too. Think about ditching the desks. By removing furniture, it maximizes the learning space for the kids so that they can work with one another and makes it easier for kids to work with partners or in small groups.

Details matter to students and student learning, and an attention to detail is a strength of the designer. Students see how things interact. They notice the subtlety of the colors, shapes, and angles. They recognize the unintended consequences of each decision. It is important that teachers grow their understanding in these ways. Some teachers are naturally talented in these areas. They have a vision for what a space can be, but others need practice to make this a lens that they wear. Teachers can practice this by thinking about the color, artwork, and flow of spaces that they pass through each day. Every visual and every movement impacts culture, attitude, and energy. By practicing the designer's mindset, teachers can enter the conversation about their learning-space transformation projects with a more trained eye and a deeper empathy.

CHAPTER
2

# Learning-Space Change as a Lever to Shift School Culture

## WHAT DOES IT FEEL LIKE?

It is difficult to measure "feel." In some ways "feel" is your gut instinct as a teacher, but it is fair to say we all "feel" something when we enter a place. Picture a time when you walked into an amusement park with a child, and within seconds, you could see the excitement and joy on his or her face. It would be nearly impossible for a school to compete with an amusement park, but it is realistic to have spaces that feel warm, welcoming, and student centered to people who enter.

When you walk into a room do you feel a vibe? Do you get a sense of the personality or of the culture? Will Rogers probably said it best when he said, "You never get a second chance to make a first impression." Keeping that in mind is critical when teachers and leaders embark on redesigning learning space. It is also key as a teacher looking to make change. What is the vision for your classroom, and does your space support that vision?

## HOW DO WE BEGIN THE CONVERSATION?

Three years ago, Warner Elementary, in Spring Arbor, Michigan looked very dull. As visitors and students entered the school, they noticed white walls, extremely dated plaques adorning those walls, floors that lacked a sparkle, and an overall blandness that didn't inspire creativity, individuality, or warmth.

During this time, the Warner staff was undergoing a transformation. The school was transitioning to become a *Leader in Me* school (FranklinCovey, n.d.), and an initial part of the process included the painting of all restrooms. It was truly magical to see teachers and staff members coming together to redesign the school. You simply could not walk through the hallways without hearing staff members talking, laughing, and bonding. To the staff, the change was more than just paint; you could see morale being lifted and the culture shifting. Teamwork was everywhere. The teachers grew closer through the process.

> It is realistic to have spaces that feel warm, welcoming, and student centered to people who enter.

One Warner teacher was ready for even more change. She brainstormed a small improvement to the entryway. She suggested painting the walls a soft yellow. At the same time, someone else suggested inviting in an art student to paint a mural in the entryway. After these first set of changes were complete, the mission was clear. This would be a school with a culture of people first. It is pretty amazing to see what can happen to a school culture when educators come together to clean, wash, and paint a building for kids.

What happened next was completely unexpected.

The Warner teachers, dedicated to building a culture of learning through learning-space design, didn't stop with the entryway and restrooms. The makeover took on a life of its own. Empowered teachers in one hallway decided to create, "Leaders Lane." Outside of each classroom, teachers painted murals. They put up light posts in the hallway with yellow painted light bulbs. The teachers' hard work gave the hallway a feel of a cozy lane inside a school. A sense of genuine pride permeated through the school. Staff members eagerly anticipated what community members and students would say about the new culture that they were creating for kids.

Then came the moment of truth. A handful of students and their parents entered the school. Staff members stopped what they were doing and watched their reaction. The teachers saw joy on students' faces, and it made all the hard work worth it. One young lady walked into the redesigned restroom and immediately you heard, "Wow!" She then mentioned the quote on the wall, the color of the new paint, and how everything shined. That summer work was a game changer, not only did the building transform in appearance, but more important, the culture and morale was at an all-time high.

Science journalist and author Emily Anthes (2009) says, "They [educators] are unearthing tantalizing clues about how to design spaces that promote creativity, keep students focused and alert, and lead to relaxation and social intimacy." Teachers who are embracing these clues are hearing comments like the following:

- "I love the natural light in the school."
- "The pictures on the walls are all students; you can see the focus is on kids."
- "The floor shines! There is a high standard when it comes to cleanliness."
- "Easy-to-read instructions let all visitors know exactly what is expected."

# HOW TO START FROM GROUND ZERO?

Many educators dream of the day that they can be a part of a brand-new building. Just imagine—abundant spaces, no leaks in the roof, a solid infrastructure, and up-to-date modern fixtures. This new opportunity to build a space that supports a healthy culture of learning does come with its own set of unique challenges.

Curt Rees, a principal in Wisconsin, recently underwent such a process. Rees provides the following suggestions for the committee of educators charged with bringing a new building online (C. Rees, personal interview, February 4, 2016):

- Read, read, and read some more to discover the ins and outs of design. Rees suggests reading *The Language of School Design, The Third Teacher,* and *Make Space.*
- Investigate architects including walking through multiple sites at which they have worked and requiring a formal presentation.
- Talk with educators who work in a building that the architects designed including asking questions like, "What would you change if you could go back?"
- Discuss ALL the spaces including traffic flow, office space, security, and infrastructure.

Rees leans on Professor John Nash from the University of Kentucky in the area of school design. Nash always starts with a question: How do you want people to feel when they use this space? Professor Nash and Rees clearly understand how emotions play a vital role in the design process. Rees and his teachers also focus on the 4 Cs: collaboration, creativity, critical thinking, and communication. The 4 Cs should serve as a point of focus when you are on the journey of designing learning spaces. Other questions to consider include the following:

- Is the learning environment safe?
- Are the colors warm and inviting?
- Is the learning space welcoming?
- Does the learning space offer flexibility?

Rees and his team worked with all stakeholders. He suggested meeting with groups and discussing these questions:

- What do you currently like about your space?
- What do you wish you could change about your space?
- What are some experiences or spaces that you have enjoyed in other schools?

Finally, Rees cautions teachers and leaders involved in this work to be patient and understand that planning and preparation takes time.

## WHY DOESN'T LEARNING HAVE TO HAPPEN IN A TRADITIONAL CLASSROOM?

Hamilton School District is taking Learning Spaces to a new level. Superintendent David Tebo and his teachers have a tremendous amount of passion for education. He

> *The 4 Cs should serve as a point of focus when you are on the journey of designing learning spaces.*

empowers staff members and gives them the green light to try new things. Tebo embraces opportunity and isn't afraid to take risks. Tebo said that he has argued for a while that if we want to take teaching and learning to the next level, we have to look at the spaces that we use to engage students (D. Tebo, personal interview, February 5, 2016).

*good argument*

For the past three years, a group of Tebo's teachers have done just that as they intentionally built learning experiences that take place outdoors. The work started when a group of passionate educators designed and built the nature-based preschool, Little Hawks Discovery Preschool, located on the grounds of the Outdoor Discovery Center Macatawa Greenway (ODC). The idea envisioned by these teachers has now expanded to the middle school where a team of two teachers works with 58 students in a half-day class that blends math, science, and a variety of elective options. The seventh grade students also have an outdoor lab space located on the grounds of the ODC.

Little Hawks students go to preschool for three hours and spend one and a half of those hours outdoors, sun, rain, or snow. During the school's short tenure, they have seen amazing things from the learners, and they have watched parents react positively as their children embrace a learning environment that some doubted would be as academically successful. One of the biggest success stories has been watching the students with special needs, especially the ones who attend an early childhood special education program in the afternoon. These students are able to succeed in ways that they haven't been able to in a traditional environment. There is no need for a sensory break or time away from the learning, because they are immersed in the learning, and their behavior has significantly improved. Learning spaces like these clearly change a learning culture and generate huge benefits for all students and teachers.

Kids are curious by nature, and in their earliest years gravitate toward being outside. Have you seen children find a mud puddle and then witness their natural joy if they are allowed to organically interact with it? The staff at Little Hawks gets to see moments like this and many more on a daily basis. They watch as students play and explore in a natural setting, and the further they get from an adult, the more confident and reliant on themselves they become. Teachers here are building a culture of self-reliance. It's amazing to watch a child with a teacher or adult in close proximity look to that adult for instructions or help and then to see the same child with no adult present and see the increase in confidence and curiosity.

When we envision learning spaces of the future what do we see? David Tebo and his teachers should be applauded for being pioneers in breaking down barriers and showing us new ways. He sees a future without walls and without restrictions. He has a vision that is refreshing to hear.

## WHAT ARE THE POTENTIAL STEPS TO BEGIN THE REDESIGN?

Before you begin to shape a school's culture through space design, it is critical to have a shared vision. Ask teachers and others questions like, "What does your school stand for? Does everyone in the organization believe in the vision?" Build a brand for your school that includes things like logo, motto, hashtag, and more. Begin the conversation about a potential makeover of the spaces of the school. Listen to people's thoughts and opinions through a lens of culture change, and remember, it is essential for this to be the work of the collective whole.

Once there is a critical mass of teachers on board, it is important to start small. Focus on areas that everyone can get behind. Some examples include the entryway, library, restrooms, and cafeteria. The best results come when professionals have some freedom in the process. Empower your fellow teachers through each step of the process.

Big shifts in culture can come from low cost actions. Places to begin include adding color and paint to dull areas, tapping into community resources for local artists to paint murals, contacting a photographer to have pictures displayed throughout the hallways, finding inspirational posters to have framed and hung throughout the building, planting flowers, or walking the building with others and looking for areas that simply need attention. Don't forget about these ideas that can both transform culture and control costs.

1. Forget about looks.

   No, really, looks are not everything. Your school or district probably has tables that are in good shape, but they may not all "match." Use them! This is a terrific way to show the value of a redesign to the school and district leadership.

2. Blend new with old.

   Taking your desks and putting them into pods is an easy way to increase collaboration and teamwork. Then add to the redesign by purchasing balance/yoga balls for student seating. Another way to

   (Continued)

blend new with old is by refurbishing current furniture and painting or re-upholstering. These simple steps can make a major difference to the feel of your space.

3. Get handy!

   It will cost you time, a bit of money, and possibly your own sweat, but purchasing whiteboards and turning them into table tops can add a lot to your learning space. It is also possible to build your own bookshelves for your classroom. These handy projects increase buy-in and often become a source of pride in the learning space.

4. Take one step at a time.

   Redesign is a journey. It takes time and planning. Think of your entire classroom, is there one area where you can start? A reading nook? A mini-maker space? A writer's station? If funding or time is limited, you should focus on one area to begin the redesigning journey.

## HOW SHOULD WE SHOWCASE THE REDESIGN?

Once a space has been overhauled, it is only the beginning of the cultural transformation as additional benefits come from showcasing the changes publicly. Typically, this begins with family, friends, and colleagues checking out the changes, but there are additional ways to increase foot traffic. The obvious is a back-to-school night or open house that features the hard work of the teachers and staff, but there are even more ways to build positive climate.

Consider leaving a space for students to continue to work with, and then invite the community in to support the students in completing the space. This can be an inspiration wall where students put their colored hand prints on the wall or an outdoor space where families can assist with assembly and manual labor. Doing this supports culture building and enhances the work of the teachers. This allows the community to feel part of the school in a more hands-on way.

It is also essential to showcase the school's progress through social media. Many educators know the value of sharing their story. Teachers and leaders should share before-and-after photos of redesign projects on social media as well. Take pictures of students using the learning spaces. This will help with future opportunities to shift spaces and grow culture, and it is a nice way to share the great things happening in classrooms.

Leading building tours allows teachers and leaders to show off the school to families. Discuss the redesign and the vision for all students to succeed. There is nothing better than face-to-face conversations. Allow visiting families to feel the culture and climate of the building while school is in session.

Invite university and college professors into the school. Educate them on the importance of learning spaces. Never miss an opportunity to showcase the school. By showcasing your school and its learning spaces people will feel valued, and it will lift the culture of the building.

CHAPTER
3

# Shaping Learning-Space Change for the Community

In John Hardy's 2010 TEDGlobal Talk, he shared with the world a "Green School Dream" for the future. Hardy's dream became a reality in 2008 when he and his wife opened the Green School in Bali, Indonesia. The Green School was different from traditional schools because of its emphasis on design, environment, and a pedagogical connection to the learning space. The Green School's vision, mission, and values all connect to the power of space.

The Green School vision, as stated at www.greenschool.org, "is of a natural, holistic, student-centered learning environment that empowers and inspires our students to be creative, innovative, green leaders." This vision allows for all learners, both students and adults, to stay in tune with the beauty of the space that surrounds them.

They use this vision to propel their mission of "educating young leaders in global citizenship. . . . champion a new model of learning that connects the timeless lessons from nature to a relevant and effective preparation for a fast-changing future."

With a clear vision and mission, the Green School was able to develop a common set of values that is seen throughout their dedication to learning embedded in their space. They "believe in three simple rules underlying every decision: be local; let your environment be your guide; and envisage how your grandchildren will be affected by your actions."

The environment impacts and drives the curriculum at various levels of learning. Students use every inch of the interior and exterior space for learning experiences, places to collaborate, as well as opportunities to make and create.

When we share the story of the Green School in Bali with teachers, we usually get the same response: That's nice, but we could never do that. We have limitations that keep us from overhauling the entire space to make a connection to the curriculum and learning as they have in Bali.

And they are right to think that.

So the question is, does that mean we forget about the impact learning-space design has on students, teachers, and the entire community?

## ARE SHIFTING LEARNING SPACES A GATEWAY TO SHIFTING THE COMMUNITY AT LARGE?

A 2001 study by the International Interior Design Association (IIDA) found that *92 percent of teachers* believe classroom design has a strong impact on students' learning and achievement. The study goes on to state the following:

> These statistics demonstrate that teachers believe there may be a direct link between classroom design and student

performance. In fact, ninety-nine percent of the survey respondents believe that school design is important for creating a good learning environment in their classrooms, eighty-nine percent believe it is important for teacher retention, and seventy-nine percent believe it is important for student attendance. Students and teachers spend most of their time in school, and logic tells us that interior design should be important to them for making their school experience a positive one. (SchoolFacilities.com, 2001)

Do you believe this? Do you acknowledge this as teachers and leaders of change?

*Study*

In a 2012 pilot study by the University of Salford and architects, Nightingale Associates, it was found that the classroom environment can affect a child's academic progress over a year by as much as 25 percent.

Yes, you read that correctly—25 percent!

Yet, we continue to focus on many other areas when it comes to student achievement and growth. We continue to put space and environment on the back burner, while

> Classroom environment can affect a child's academic progress over a year by as much as 25 percent.

other areas dominate our time and attention. We forget that making a difference is about the small changes we make, day after day, week after week, month after month in our schools, and learning-space design needs to be part of that work.

*One message*

If this book has one message, it's simple: Learning spaces matter and they impact the entire teaching and learning community.

Yet, we make the case (and research supports) that learning spaces also impact

- A classroom culture
- A school culture
- The entire community

If a classroom or learning space has broken chairs, old desks, uncomfortable seating arrangements, lack of light, and defaced walls . . . then something must be done immediately. When a learning space is transformed into a place where the design is not hindering student learning, we begin to see a shift in the classroom culture.

This notion of spaces directly affecting community and culture is similar to the ways citizens respond with the *broken window effect*.

In a March 1982 article in *The Atlantic Monthly* titled *Broken Windows*, the broken window theory is explained:

> Consider a building with a few broken windows. If the windows are not repaired, the tendency is for vandals to break a few more windows. Eventually, they may even break into the building, and if it's unoccupied, perhaps become squatters or light fires inside.
>
> Or consider a section of pavement. Some litter accumulates. Soon, more litter accumulates. Eventually, people even start leaving bags of refuse from take-out restaurants there or even break into cars.
>
> A number of studies have been done on the broken window effect to demonstrate what happens when the windows are fixed and the pavement is clean. In turn, citizens do not deface the building or throw trash on the ground. Their environment shapes actions, just as the actions impact the environment. (Kelling, 1982)

Have you questioned the following in your classroom?

- How do my students respond to the spaces in our classroom?
- Is there a sense of pride and community around our space?
- Is there a difference between the way students connect and collaborate in my classroom versus in the hallway?
- Can I take our classroom from a space, to a place, to a home?

The last question is the most important. Is your current classroom a space? A place? Or a home for your students? The difference between these words will signal to students whether or not they can have a deeper sense of community and belonging in your classroom.

## HOW ARE THE COMMUNITY AND THE SCHOOLS THE SAME ECOSYSTEM?

Innovative learning-space design must include access to intentional green space on the grounds of the school and throughout the community. Even in urban areas where green space isn't plentiful, learning must not be contained to the classroom. World leaders and solution-based thinkers haven't and won't develop their best ideas from a classroom desk. Idea-generating students come from robust interactions with the world. This means touching the soil, speaking with other adult experts, and noticing the small things that surround them. ✳

Learning spaces that accentuate the opportunity to interact with the community speak without speaking that the true mission for students lies beyond the walls of the schools. Many teachers are already doing this by embracing outdoor classrooms, having students spend time away from school grounds, and allowing kids to scatter throughout the school grounds in an attempt to make deep learning connections.

Redesigning learning spaces without a culture of creating leaves so much potential at the door. This makes it essential for teachers to couple learning-space transformation with work to encourage meaningful maker learning. Maker education, with its focus on creating, making, and designing around student passions, has become a topic of great interest among many. They see this type of learning as a path toward deeper, more integrated college and career readiness. They see students involved in maker education as more engaged and connected to their schools and community. They see an opportunity to reignite the tuned-out students and lower the dropout rate.

The maker movement and the teachers who make it possible need the right spaces to be successful. This includes things like

- increasing power supplies in rooms,
- sturdy tables for constructing, and
- storage that keeps expensive tools safe and protected.

Learning spaces that support maker education aren't all about the furniture though. They also include space for the ideation and prototyping phases of design thinking. Teachers should see maker education housed in the right learning habitat as a focus on quality instruction that allows kids to be passionate about learning and grow as productive citizens and leaders in their communities.

## HOW CAN LEARNING-SPACE SHIFTS AND THE GREATER COMMUNITY SUPPORT KIDS EMOTIONALLY?

Isn't it amazing the energy that comes from a stage? Each year, the performing arts centers of most high schools in the country showcase kids doing incredible things. They showcase harmony in voice, the power of orchestra, and the emotion-shifting power of a quality band. They highlight students performing as dancers, singers, and actors or actresses. The stage is truly a golden place for so many students. These highlights are captured in a set of images that spread across the community in both traditional media and all of the modern media platforms. The evenings of performances are community celebrations, and leaders are there to see the best moments of the year. What would it look like for all of our classrooms to feel like performing arts spaces?

- Could we celebrate chemistry the same way we clap for the cha cha?
- Could we applaud history as though the orchestra had just played Haydn?
- Could literature feel like an evening at the theater?

As we construct new learning spaces, it is important to consider how space brings energy and attitude. Quality spaces can bring a feeling of deep worth to parts of a school system that too often ranks its favorite things by its shiny outcomes.

## WHAT STEPS ARE NECESSARY FOR EFFECTIVE COMMUNICATION TO THE COMMUNITY ABOUT INNOVATION IN LEARNING-SPACE DESIGN?

Connecting to the community at large is an important piece of the re-envisioned learning-space puzzle. Making changes in classrooms that ultimately benefit the entire community may seem like an unnecessary expense to some communities. To other communities, they may only notice the aesthetic differences and applaud the change in space for looks (instead of the connection to teaching, learning, culture, and community building).

If you only bring the community into the discussion about learning-space redesign when the conversation is about funds and money, then you've already lost them.

Here is a quick step-by-step guide to effective communication to the community about innovation in learning-space design:

- Back-to-school or open house night is a perfect place for the discussion to begin. Most schools have these nights in the beginning of the year. Make sure to emphasize what the current space design is and the limitations. Have a place where teachers, students, leaders, and parents can all discuss the future of learning spaces at the school.

- Create a "street" team of parents, students, teachers, and leaders interested in learning-space design. Committees tend to sit around and talk, while teams take action and get to work. Schedule two to four school visits with the street team to see other innovative learning spaces.

- Live stream and video the learning spaces at the other schools. Make sure the visit is not just for the street team but that anyone can access the footage on the school website, Twitter account, Facebook page, and so on.

- Host a town hall meeting (could happen at a school board meeting) where the street team members will present their findings, research, and possibilities for change. Invite the community to ask questions, and, above all else, get them excited.

- The next stage of the process will ultimately be decided by funds, and it is important to have the street team, school, and community rallied around the cause at this point in time.

- Once plans for a redesign are finalized, put together a video for the community that shows the new design and gives a date for the changes to happen.

- Have a celebration! Invite the community to celebrate along with the school as the redesign takes place. If it is one classroom, invite the parents, and throw a party. If it is a larger space, make sure to acknowledge the hard work of those on the street team, and talk about the community's involvement throughout the process.

Each school and community is different, but the key is to involve, inspire, and excite all the stakeholders around learning-space design and its impact on the community.

CHAPTER

4

# Learning Space as a Lever for Systemic Change

## HOW DO SMALL MOMENTS HAVE BIG IMPACT ON SYSTEMS?

Over the last few years, it has become obvious that overall systems change in education is only possible when there are a handful of champions throughout an organization who can keep the change energy and momentum alive. This remains true when it comes to the powerful opportunities for systems change that can come from intentional adjustments to learning spaces. Work around learning-space design rarely makes a dent in changing the learning or adding joy to school without strong teachers advocating for excellence in this area. Only with a true understanding about the potential impact of quality learning spaces can change really scale through a learning system. Certainly there may be a few showplaces in each school that have a teacher or leader with a designer's heart, but only when a critical mass of teachers is missional in this work can it be threaded together into a series of actions that can leverage deep changes in learning for all kids.

*Portable, flexible,* and *agile* are some of the adjectives central to this work to transform learning spaces from factory model schemes to modern educational ecosystems. These are actually concepts that are needed to modernize other systems in education as well, but education as a system is slow to move, slow to innovate, and slow to realize that its practices are failing. These struggles to modernize are amplified by a world beyond the realm of education that continues to innovate and advance at an increasing pace and that doesn't appear to be stopping soon. This means that schools are functioning well below the pace of society, and thus they are struggling to prepare kids in the area of career readiness without bringing a culture that is portable, flexible, and agile to the forefront. Teachers who recognize this flaw in our system can be instrumental in being a voice for change.

The children headed to success in the next century will be both creative and curious. They will be citizens who can devise solutions and care deeply. These essential growth areas will be strengthened when students have been in learning spaces throughout their school career that foster these traits and others. The ideal spaces will nurture student choice and voice and bring authentic audience into the learning.

Learning spaces must echo the energy, pace, and intensity of the world around education. When students are exposed to a world that fails forward fast, they realize that iteration, risk taking, and the process of unlearning and relearning are essential elements of success. It is also important that our most innovative teachers feel this same way.

Innovative learning spaces facilitate this modern learning that can keep pace with the complexity of career and passion fields. These spaces amplify creativity and curiosity in ways unheard of in classrooms stricken by fixed rows. Can we actually think of a greater symbol of the broken school than classrooms with fixed rows and desks that are stuck to the wax from the summer? In too many places though, this factory line approach to learning, that attempts a linear acquisition of knowledge that is delivered by one expert, is the norm. This reality haunts our best teachers. They recognize the need for change. In addition, these old learning spaces remove joy and energy from the classroom. They are energy vampires that result in heads on desks, kids sleeping, and the adults doing all of the learning.

"In every deliberation, we must consider the impact of our decisions on the next seven generations." This quote from the great law of the Iroquois Confederacy speaks into something that is lacking in most school change. It is essential for teachers in conjunction with their leaders to think about sustainability of their proposed changes including changes in learning spaces. The needs of students today won't be the same tomorrow, but the changes today may need to last for seven generations.

Many educators, though, get caught chasing new shiny things. This mindset results in maintaining traditional systems, jumping to new systems, and pushing old systems into shiny new cases. One of the issues that contribute to this is that there is rarely time for groups of teachers to talk about sustainable practices based on a vision shared by many and implemented by most. With learning spaces, this means considering not only how the classroom will look different next year but also how it will look different five years later and five years after that. Because as teachers and facilitators of learning, we can never allow another stretch of time when something like rows and heavy desks infect our classroom spaces for so long.

Redesigning spaces to maximize learning is primarily a shift in culture and mindset. For a teacher leading change, this means building a showcase in one space, so that a cascade of interest, energy, and excitement can ripple across the system. One learning space is a stake in the ground that the old way of learning where classrooms feel like cemeteries (imagine desks as head stones) and prisons (trapped in one place all day) are truly leaving the system.

Over and over, we see the first space that shifts becomes a cultural trigger that has educators asking whether they can be next and whether it can be tomorrow.

When a teacher changes her or his learning space, it means a commitment to student-centered learning including a shift in the locus of control. Too many spaces of learning have a central place of information dissemination. It is the place where 90% of time the teacher is located for 90% of their lessons. This legacy location in a room is a structural barrier to the shifts needed for successful learning-space transformation. It is this location that prevents out-of-the-box thinking. It is this location that sends the message that learning happens when the teacher is talking. It is in this location where student voice, exploration, and serendipitous learning is thwarted.

Flexible learning spaces can expose control-based classroom management systems employed by teachers. All innovative work in schools produces unintended consequences. Some of these are positive while others create challenges. Flexible learning spaces amplify the impact of poor teaching, and this is especially true when a classroom facilitator manages through control. Learning-space shifts aren't alone in exposing marginal practices in classrooms. We also see this with the introduction of technology and when unclear learning objectives and targets are in place for students. The reason that this happens with learning-space changes is that as the amount of student-centered time increases, and as students control the flow, pace, and direction of the class, more and more legacy practices fail.

This is an unstoppable force that left to its own devices creates a situation where struggling teachers are thrust forward into a bright light that exposes practices that are ineffective. The result of this is that some teachers can push back against learning-space design changes in the name of self-preservation because no one wants their weaknesses exposed publicly. It is essential for innovative teachers to support their colleagues in these moments of disequilibrium and provide ideas and resources on how to shift their daily practices to support learning in their modern habitat.

## HOW CAN WE THINK ABOUT LEARNING SPACES AS DEEP LEVERS OF CHANGE?

Most of our best teachers have recognized that something needs to be done to change the current reality around learning spaces. They want classrooms that get kids excited and engaged in their work, but in too many places, we are seeing shifts in learning spaces based on areas of convenience instead of areas of highest impact. We see this with new benches being donated for the front of a school or a new playground (playgrounds are definitely learning spaces) by the parent organization. These additions to beautify learning spaces often result in schools stopping with just these superficial changes because there is no vision for how to use smaller chunks of funding in a coherent way to achieve meaningful results.

This leads to purchases that add to the aesthetics but have no strategic impact on real learning. In so many places, parents, potential partners, and donors move so much more quickly than the school is used to making decisions that it creates suboptimal results. Groups of teachers, serving as a voice for building, need to be thinking about how they will strategically use the next $50, $500, $5000, and $50,000 infusion of funds. With this level of forethought, learning-space design can be available and powerful for all no matter their budget.

The entry points for teachers and classrooms into the meaningful shifts in learning through space design are numerous. For some, it is about flexible seating. For others, it is about writeable surfaces, and for others, it is taking the first steps to moving from a classroom full of rows of desks to fresh options. Don't overlook how powerful foundational items like lighting, acoustics, and air quality can be as they quietly set the tone for the daily teaching and learning in schools.

As one grows as a teacher who sees through this systems lens around learning spaces, it will become obvious how essential elements of space design like lighting, acoustics, and air quality are controlled by the people removed from the learning process. This often looks like incredibly passionate, caring maintenance, custodial, and buildings and grounds directors making a remarkable number of decisions around the health, well-being, and learning of kids.

To best support your students and their learning, carefully look at other systems as well including, how budgets are used to refresh furniture, whose voices surround construction projects, the process to buy supplies, and the decisions on how to prioritize work orders. It takes a seasoned educational lens that comes from years of serving kids and adults in areas of curriculum, instruction, and assessment to connect the dots and thread together a meaningful learning-space design strategy. It is a healthy culture that allows aspects of learning-space design to penetrate in all places of learning including new spaces, renovated spaces, and current spaces that need adjustments because of an inherent risk or potential harm.

## IN WHAT WAYS CAN TEACHERS BLEND LEARNING-SPACE DESIGN AND TECHNOLOGY INTEGRATION TO MAXIMIZE CHANGE ACROSS THE SYSTEM?

Learning-space shifts are often coupled with the introduction of technology into a school district. Though this coupling makes sense because both are potential positive disruptions to the system, neither requires the other, yet both can amplify the power that each can have on the learning ecosystem. Connected classrooms work most efficiently with a learning habitat that matches the innovative possibilities of technology infusion. Painting a crumbling house or going through the car wash with a vehicle in need of a transmission are both recipes for failure. Schools that are bringing the characteristics of excellent technology infusion to their classroom are often doing so with no forethought around the minimal impact that the technology tools will have without a learning space that supports engaged, empowered learning.

Braiding together excellent educational habitats with the power of mobile, ubiquitous technology can transform learning as we know it. Using the word *habitat* for our classrooms doesn't always fit comfortably for many teachers, but the truth is that learning spaces that do excellent things for kids do look, sound, and feel like habitats. They envelop the learners freeing them from things like bullying, hunger, and stress. When these supportive learning habitats feature the right light, sound, and color, and they are coupled with flexible seating, writable spaces, studio space, and space to celebrate hard work, students feel their inner power to learn magnified.

History tells us that we are quickly approaching the fad stage for learning-space design. It has the potential to follow the pattern of most educational waves of change that result in high-cost, low-impact results. Teachers who want to help avoid this in their classrooms should look to the last decade around technology integration for wisdom. In doing so, they will see that success requires a laser focus on meaningful shifts in pedagogy. Without this focus, there will definitely be low impact, high-cost spaces emerging because the focus will be on the stuff instead of on the stuff that makes learning great.

In a time when the amount of visual data consumed by students each day continues to grow in geometric ways, and students are using YouTube as their primary search engine, it is essential to weave visually stimulating learning into schools in a deeper way. This flood of visuals consumed by students makes the realities of many of our current classrooms, which are devoid of color, design, and visual stimulation, an unpalatable contrast. This doesn't mean that learning-space design should overstimulate or parallel the visual frenzy of life for students, but teachers need to acknowledge that the eighteen hours a day beyond school can't be left at the classroom door when it comes to supporting learners through the maze of the visual society.

> Success requires a laser focus on meaningful shifts in pedagogy.

Technology integration is allowing students to have the tools to grow as videographers and digital storytellers. Student voice is showcasing the mission of the school in a way that no adult message is able to resonate. To promote this, teachers are converting learning spaces into studios that facilitate audio and video creation. This includes the introduction of green screen technology, small sections of the room that are designed to record high quality audio, studio spaces for editing, and raised spaces for students to present to peers. All of these shifts in learning spaces are allowing the genuine learning stories of the classroom to resonate to taxpayers, local business, and beyond.

Technology use in flexible learning spaces requires more thought and planning than ever before but can produce the greatest results, both short and long term for kids. Technology-rich spaces, when coupled with thoughtful learning-space design, can be a catalyst for exciting change. As a teacher looking to make change in this way, consider the following questions:

- Are learning goals deep in nature, so that technology and learning spaces can root within them? This means that learning units need fresh energy spread into them. Old units done in beautiful spaces with excellent tools will plateau.

- Does the technology flexibility mirror the learning-space design flexibility? Desktops, computers, and huge carts in beautiful learning spaces inhibit their potential before they are launched. Technology that doesn't feature creation tools like cameras and video- and audio-editing apps won't support excellent habitats of learning.

- How does the community view technology usage? If it is unnoticed or a burden on the system, then more than likely the efforts around learning-space design (as they are relatives in innovation) will be seen the same way.

## HOW CAN TEACHERS BEST USE THEIR RESOURCES TO CREATE SYSTEMIC CHANGE?

Transforming learning spaces is currently seen as an expensive initiative, but the reality is that it can be done without finding a money tree. Smart, precise decisions by teachers who are focused on the purpose of their learning space can bring substantial, affordable change. Design work though isn't an intuitive strength for teachers, but all humans are designers, and with a focus on students and their needs as foundational to the process, quick wins can emerge.

These wins include bringing new options in lighting, seating, work spaces, and idea-generating spaces for students. With these success stories, a formula can emerge that allows other teachers throughout the building and district to replicate the success. This formula includes spending some money early, studying the student and teacher behaviors that emerge in the new spaces, then making a bulk of the purchases based on this feedback. As a final piece to the plan, use a smaller remaining part of the budget to supplement the things that are successful to truly amplify the impact of the learning-space project.

Teachers who have used this system in their work as leaders and change agents have also been able to support three larger systemic changes. The first is a pattern of partnership. Teachers need partners. Many teachers do this, but they embrace it at a surface level and fail to engage in deep partnership. Deep partnership often looks like learning in spaces beyond the school in places like coworking spaces, government buildings, and industry headquarters. As teachers are innovative about where students learn, it frees up classroom spaces to become performance spaces, design centers, and idea studios. Learning-space design requires seeing every community space as an opportunity. In doing so, budgets aren't busted, and new experts are infused into the learning.

The second systemic change that teachers can support is a laser focus on meaningful learning. More and more people are being inspired to create, make, and design new classroom spaces based on Pinterest. All of these pins have created an explosion of ideas that are often dumped into a space like the paint splattered on canvas by Jackson Pollock. The result is a classroom museum of lots of cool things that can be reposted and celebrated but that lacks the impact on learning to justify the time and money spent.

Meaningful change is about deep shifts in how students receive learning, so lead classroom design with purpose. In order to maintain a focus on learning, teachers should promote a culture that has continuous conversations about the principles of excellent learning. It also includes asking tough questions about the choices being made. Teachers who promote a culture of asking questions create more learning, more understanding, and a greater expansion of how and why space design matters.

The final systemic change that teachers can support is thinking about all spaces as potential places for excellent learning. An example is hallways. They are untapped resources for learning-space design. Almost half of all school spaces are found outside of the traditional learning space (classrooms), and teachers can leverage these nontraditional learning spaces. Hallways are ideal places for collaborative work, ideation stations featuring writable surfaces, television displays that showcase and celebrate school successes, and comfortable, quiet seating options that support the needs of introverts throughout the day.

Hallways are often the spaces most travelled by visitors to the building, which leaves them ripe for telling the story and mission of the school based on the intentionality of their design. Hallways lacking intentional design also speak volumes to visitors about the type of learning and dedication to caring that is happening in the building even if it is only based on this limited perception. Teachers can play a large role in supporting the school through creative, innovative use of the hallway spaces.

## WHO ELSE IS SUPPORTING THIS WORK TO CHANGE LEARNING THROUGH SPACE DESIGN?

As classroom teachers looking to make innovative classroom change for your space and the overall spaces throughout the school, it is good to know that this work is being supported throughout the system of education. From the classroom, it is often difficult to know if best practices and innovative ideas are being supported with resources, conversations, and influence from the highest levels. In the area of learning-space design, it is clear that many are seeing great value.

Since 2011, the United States Department of Education has supported the Green Ribbon Schools Program (U.S. Department of Education, 2015). This program has helped to shape the narrative about school design and ideal learning spaces for kids. In addition, it has shined a bright light on the fact that too many students attend schools each day with inhibiting factors like lead paints, poor air quality, cleaning materials with fumes and vapors, poor lighting, and substandard acoustics. Learning-space designers have to assure that these areas are in place before innovation and excellent, beautiful learning spaces can be built.

To support this, the Green Ribbon Schools Program has built out an incredible group of resources from the Department of Education, the Environmental Protection Agency, and the Department of Energy that supports the complexity of modernizing learning spaces. The resources focus on reducing environmental impact on learning, improving health and wellness, and supporting sustainable education. All elements, when unpacked, are issues inherently nested in the work of modern space design.

The Green Ribbon Schools award winners are also excellent exemplars that teachers can use to build model processes and structures for transformation. Groups of teachers are also using these resources, ideas, and inspiration to forge partnerships with local parks and recreation, community center spaces, design professionals in the area, local businesses, and church groups. These conversations vary in nature as each community has unique needs, but a common thread has been about how schools can use these community areas as they often sit empty during normal school hours.

Another key resource in the movement to revolutionize learning spaces is the work emerging from the Future Ready Schools Initiative. During the fall of 2014, President Obama called on educators to look more critically at their work to build and scale change (The WhiteHouse.gov, 2014). He called on teachers and leaders to use their voice to engage all stakeholders in conversations about the changes needed for schools to truly be future ready. A learning initiative at its core, Future Ready seeks to provide greater equity and excellence in education that is lacking in many places. Unlike some ideas that come from a national level that are received with a lukewarm reception, the Future Ready Initiative has been seen as deep and significant work, celebrated and validated by thousands through their signing of the Future Ready Pledge.

The resources of the Future Ready Schools Initiative include a dashboard that allows schools to assess their current readiness based on a set of criteria known as gears. The dashboard also showcases examples of other schools that are achieving success. Other benefits of the process for teachers include opening new perspectives on how curriculum, instruction, and assessment are all bolstered with a more student-centered classroom design.

# Models of Excellence and a Place to Start

Teachers are agents of change. They impact students' lives in ways that are sometimes seen but most often unseen. They guide, help, inspire, challenge, and care for students. This happens through conversations, teachable moments, small group work, full class discussion, and many more daily interactions.

But what if educators could impact the learning in classrooms and schools by focusing on what learning spaces look like, how they function, and what purpose they serve?

What if this change positively impacted students, the community, and the culture of a school?

Hopefully by this point in the book you are shouting out a resounding, "Yes! We need to do this!"

And the truth is, there are many different ways to go about doing this. Some involve bootstrapping the learning-space design by yourself, others include administrative support or community buy in, but often, all it takes is an idea, a connection, and the guts to go out there and make it happen.

## WHO IS DOING THIS WELL?

Matt Miller is a teacher at Cascade Middle School in Clayton, Indiana. Last summer Matt was on a date night with his wife when they decided to swing into an Orange Leaf Frozen Yogurt restaurant for some sweets.

While waiting, Matt began to look at the people who had already received their yogurt. They were chatting, laughing, and eating. Stories were being told. Each group was having their own conversation, but no one was being so loud that it bothered any other group.

There were multiple tables. Each surrounded by four chairs that looked really comfortable. There were a couple of sets of couches facing each other. Each area had been specifically placed to allow groups of four to look at each other.

And then it hit him: Orange Leaf had better learning spaces than he did in his classroom.

So Matt tweeted out this message:

**Matt Miller**
@dropstepdunk

I'd love for my classroom to resemble an @myorangeleaf store. Would love their furniture in my classroom.

7:22 PM - 9 Aug 2015

https://twitter.com/dropstepdunk/status/630564784044421120

Little did he know that Orange Leaf headquarters would see it and reply with an offer to transform his classroom. Matt's principal at

Cascade Middle School, Eric Sieferman, received word of what happened and began talks with the powers that be.

A couple months later, with the amazing help of Orange Leaf and the Cascade Middle School parent-teacher organization (PTO), a large semi-load of furniture arrived. All in all, about eleven classrooms have some sort of Orange Leaf furniture in their rooms. Matt received three table groups (four seats apiece) and two high top tables (two seats apiece, or some students have liked to use them as standing desks).

Miller said, "Besides the generosity, kindness, and just downright awesomeness of Orange Leaf, one other really neat thing stood out, the impact of Twitter. It connects. I live in Indiana. Orange Leaf is headquartered in Oklahoma City. 750 miles away. How did this happen? A simple tweet saying that furniture like that would be really neat. Boom. It happened. How powerful is that?!"

And now the power of connections and teachers serving as agents of change is impacting his classroom and the entire school.

While this story may seem like it could never happen, similar things are happening elsewhere.

The amazing teachers at the Upper Perkiomen School District in Pennsylvania had a similar vision for a makerspace where students could build anything they could dream up. They spent a few days after school coming up with a plan, building out the specs of the "xLab" and then creating pathways for students who were traditionally in industrial arts class to go through a Maker Academy.

What did they do to make this happen?

They went to local vendors and companies looking for any type of donation. They started small, bringing in community leaders who specialized in robotics, then continued to grow by partnering with organizations like the local YMCA where students would help build benches for their new site.

By the time the teachers pitched the idea and plan to the school board, it was already in motion. The board jumped at the chance to support a project that was already positively impacting the students, the school, and the community.

In order for this to work in other places, you have to take action. You have to start before you are ready, and you've got to learn along the way. There are so many places that can support your work and give you guidance.

## WHO CAN SUPPORT YOUR WORK? WHERE CAN YOU START?

ClassroomCribs.com was created as a place for teachers and leaders to share their learning spaces and reimagine what they could look like in schools. Classroom Cribs is a hub for brain friendly learning spaces. The mission at Classroom Cribs is to enhance pedagogy and the learning experience with brain-based classroom designs that students will love. And that is the main point. We can (and should) create better learning environments for students—spaces that are centered around research and what works.

Since launching in 2014, ClassroomCribs.com has featured many brain-friendly learning spaces and transformed classrooms. It also runs a yearly design challenge where teachers share videos and photos of their learning-space projects.

But this is not the only place where you can get support for your work. Visit the accompanying website for this book to find support on

- Learning-space design
- Books on learning spaces and interior design
- Brain-friendly resources
- Funding sources and websites like DonorsChoose.com
- Research to enhance and support your redesign

You can also find a lively group of educators on Twitter sharing their work around learning spaces using the #classroomcribs hashtag!

## WHY BE AN AGENT OF CHANGE?

*Never doubt that a small group of thoughtful, committed citizens can change the world; indeed, it's the only thing that ever has.*

—Margaret Mead

We want to leave you with this final question: What can you do to be an agent of change for your students, for your school, and for your community?

We want you to be brave enough to take an idea and turn it into something tangible from which your students will benefit. Be brave enough to reach out to administration, local companies, and organizations for help and support. Be brave enough to connect with teachers and leaders around the world, and be brave enough to find a small group of committed educators that will change your students' world.

Lead change now. We can't wait to support you and share your work!

# References

Anthes, E. (2009). How room designs affect your work and mood: Brain research can help us craft spaces that relax, inspire, awaken, comfort and heal. *Scientific American.* Retrieved from http://www.scientificamerican .com/article/building-around-the-mind/

Carnegie Mellon University. (2014). *Disruptive decorations.* Retrieved from http://www.cmu.edu/homepage/society/2014/spring/disruptive-deco rations.shtml

Dutton, D. (2010). A Darwinian theory of beauty. *Ted Talks.* Retrieved from https://www.ted.com/talks/denis_dutton_a_darwinian_theory_of_ beauty?language=en

FranklinCovey. (n.d.). The leader in me. Retrieved from http://www.thelea derinme.org

Hardy, J. (2010). My green school dream. *TEDGlobal Talk.* Retrieved from https://www.ted.com/talks/john_hardy_my_green_school_dream

Kelling, G. (1982). Broken windows: The police and neighborhood safety. *Atlantic Monthly.* Retrieved from http://www.theatlantic.com/magazine/ archive/1982/03/broken-windows/304465

Kovalik, S. (n.d.). *Highly effective teaching education model.* Retrieved from http://www.thecenter4learning.com/html/resources/hetmodel.htm

SchoolFacilities.com. (2001). *Teacher's opinions about interior design and learn-ing.* Retrieved from http://www.schoolfacilities.com/_coreModules/con tent/contentDisplay_print.aspx?contentID=63

University of Salford. (2012). *Study proves classroom design really does matter.* Retrieved from http://www.salford.ac.uk/built-environment/about-us/ news-and-events/news/study-proves-classroom-design-really-does-matter

U.S. Department of Education. (2015). *U.S. Department of Education Green Ribbon Schools.* Retrieved from http://www2.ed.gov/programs/green-ribbon-schools/ index.html

The WhiteHouse.gov. (2014). *FACT SHEET: ConnectED to the future.* Retrieved from https://www.whitehouse.gov/the-press-office/2014/11/19/fact-sheet-connected-future

A SAGE Publishing Company

Helping educators make the greatest impact

**CORWIN HAS ONE MISSION:** to enhance education through intentional professional learning.

We build long-term relationships with our authors, educators, clients, and associations who partner with us to develop and continuously improve the best evidence-based practices that establish and support lifelong learning.

# Solutions you want. Experts you trust. Results you need.

### AUTHOR CONSULTING

**Author Consulting**

On-site professional learning with sustainable results! Let us help you design a professional learning plan to meet the unique needs of your school or district. www.corwin.com/pd

### INSTITUTES

**Institutes**

Corwin Institutes provide collaborative learning experiences that equip your team with tools and action plans ready for immediate implementation. www.corwin.com/institutes

### ECOURSES

**eCourses**

Practical, flexible online professional learning designed to let you go at your own pace. www.corwin.com/ecourses

### READ2EARN

**Read2Earn**

Did you know you can earn graduate credit for reading this book? Find out how: www.corwin.com/read2earn

Contact an account manager at (800) 831-6640 or visit **www.corwin.com** for more information.